This book may be kept

SEVEN DAYS

A fine will be charged for each day the book
is kept over time.

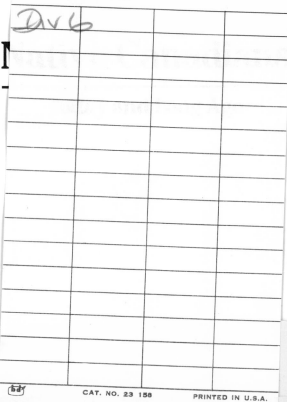

Dv6			

CAT. NO. 23 158   PRINTED IN U.S.A.

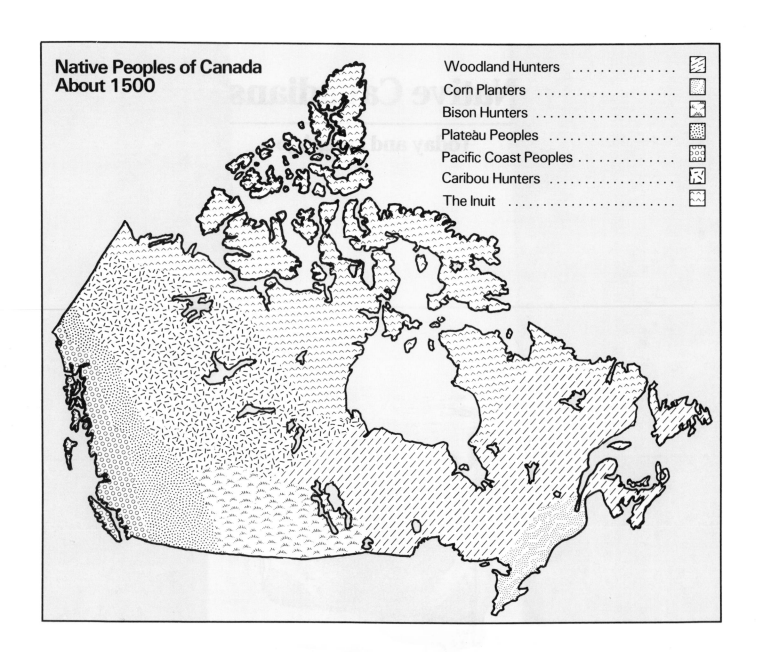

**Native Peoples of Canada
About 1500**

Woodland Hunters . . . .
Corn Planters . . . .
Bison Hunters . . . .
Plateau Peoples . . . .
Pacific Coast Peoples . . . .
Caribou Hunters . . . .
The Inuit . . . .

Native Canadians

Today and Long Ago

Elma Schemenauer

Canadian Native Peoples Series

NELSON CANADA

© Nelson Canada,
A Division of International Thomson Limited, 1985

Published in 1985 by
Nelson Canada
A Division of International Thomson Limited
1120 Birchmount Road
Scarborough, Ontario M1K 5G4

ISBN 0-17-602328-3

Canadian Cataloguing in Publication Data

Schemenauer, Elma.
    Native Canadians today and long ago

(Nelson Canadian native peoples series)
For use in elementary schools.
ISBN 0-17-602328-3

1. Indians of North America - Canada - Juvenile
literature. 2. Inuit - Canada - Juvenile literature. 1. Title. II. Series.

E78.C2S33 1985   971′.00497   C85-098016-X

Editor: Jane Lind

Design: Mary Jane Gerber

Series Consultant: David Anderson

Special thanks to Dr. Helmuth Fuchs.

The painting on page 69 is by Jackson Beardy.

Cover Illustration: Lorraine Tuson

Illustrations: Lois Andison, pages 7, 9, 11, 17, 21, 25, 27, 70,
71; Tania Craan, pages 47, 54, 55, 58, 78, 79; Ron Fyke, pages
57, 59, 60; Don Gauthier, pages 18, 19, 28, 36, 39, 73, 75, 76,
77; Nancy Kettles, pages 34, 35, 40, 41, 62, 63; Sharon
Matthews, pages 30, 32, 65, 66; Lorraine Tuson, pages 43, 44,
45, 50, 53; Paul Zwolak, page 48.

Photo Credits: PAC, page 13; Ontario Archives, page 14;
Canapress Photo Service, page 23.

1234567890/FP/0987654321

Table of Contents

Walter's People

Meeting Walter and His Family

"Come on! Let's play hockey," shouts Walter Paull. He races with his friends to the skating rink. Soon they are skating over the ice. Their dark eyes shine. The cold northern air makes their cheeks glow.

Walter and his friends live on a Woodland Cree Indian **reserve** in Northern Manitoba. Most of their houses are built of wood—boards and **plywood**. There are no fences between the houses. The people all know each other well. They like to visit and help each other. They feel that they do not need fences.

When Walter and his friends get hungry, they stop playing. As Walter walks home, he remembers that Aunt Rose and Cousin Bev will be coming from Winnipeg for the weekend. When he gets closer to his house, he smells fish frying. He knows his father caught the fish that day through holes in the ice. Fish is an important part of the diet for Walter's family in the winter.

In the winter, Walter's father is a commercial fisherman. In the summer, he and a few other men from the reserve work as tourist guides.

Walter takes off his skates and goes into his house. Sure enough, Aunt Rose and Bev have just arrived. Aunt Rose, his mother's sister, gives Walter a big hug. "How are you, Walter?" she asks.

"Fine. I scored a goal just before I came in," Walter answers.

"Good for you," Aunt Rose says.

"Do you want to watch the hockey game with us tomorrow night on TV?" Walter asks?

"I wouldn't miss it," Aunt Rose answers. "Walter, I think you have grown taller again. It's so good to see you. Bev and I get lonesome for all of you."

Aunt Rose and Bev have lived in Winnipeg for almost a year. They moved there because Aunt Rose needed a job. She could not find a job on the reserve. She is a doctor's receptionist in Winnipeg.

"I like my job," Aunt Rose says. "I like the people I work with, but I miss everyone on the reserve. Living in the city is different from living here."

"It seems so quiet here," Bev says. "I'm used to the noise in the city now."

"We sure have noise," says Aunt Rose. "An all-night donut shop opened up across the street from our apartment. Some nights there's a lot of noise over there."

Grandma asks, "Why is the store open all night? Everyone should be home sleeping."

"I agree," Aunt Rose nods, "but it seems some people in the city don't sleep at night."

"Sometimes we go to the movies on Friday or Saturday nights. That's what I like," says Bev.

"I would like the movies, too," Walter says, "and the donut shop. I'm hungry right now."

"Let's eat," Walter's mother says. She and Grandma have cooked a big fish supper.

As they go to the table, Grandma puts her arms around Bev. "How is the big city school?" Grandma asks.

"I didn't like it at first. I do now because I got used to it, and I have some friends," Bev replies.

Walter asks, "What's it like?"

"The things we study are not so different from our school here," answers Bev. "It's after school that's different. The school is so big that I don't know most of the kids."

"At our school we are working on a big play," Walter tells Bev. "Everyone on the reserve will be invited."

"What kind of play?" she asks.

"It's all about our history, and the explorers," Walter

answers. "We are going to have pow-wow dancing, too."

"I wish I could be here for your play." Bev looks at her mother.

"We can't come back too often," Aunt Rose reminds Bev. "Plane fare is expensive. It costs more to live in the city," she adds.

The only way to reach Walter's reserve is by plane. No roads go that far North. The people still get a lot of their food by hunting and fishing, as their people did long ago. Of course, Walter and his family can buy many things at the store on the reserve. Supplies are flown in so that they can shop for whatever they need.

Other people from the reserve besides Aunt Rose have moved to the city to find jobs. Walter's parents do not plan to move. They all talk more about the difference between the city and the reserve while they eat supper.

"People in the city rush around a lot," Aunt Rose says. "They don't take enough time to visit and enjoy each other."

"I like living close to people I know," Walter's father replies. "That way we can help each other out."

Aunt Rose nods her head. "That is what we miss most about the reserve—the feeling of being close to everyone we know. People in the city don't see things the way we do. But I do like my job and Bev likes her school now."

"That's good," Grandma smiles. "I'm glad you like your school, Bev. I couldn't stand living in the city. But for you, maybe it's all right. Maybe I will surprise you and come visit you in Winnipeg."

"Yes, Grandma!" Bev bounces out of her chair.

"I'll come with you, Grandma," Walter looks eagerly at his father and mother.

"Maybe," his mother says.

His father adds, "Who knows?"

Walter's School Play

The evening of the school play has come. The play is called "Newcomers in our Land." Walter is excited. He will be the narrator and tell the story. His friends will act out the story on the stage.

Walter's parents and his grandma come to see the play. Many other people from the reserve also come. A curtain hangs across the front of the school. As the curtain opens, the audience claps.

Right out in front stands Walter. He wears a shirt and **leggings** made of moose hide. Behind Walter are more students. They are also dressed the way their people dressed long ago.

Drum music starts to play. Then Walter begins to speak. He feels nervous, but his voice is loud and clear. "For thousands of years," Walter says, "our people were the only ones living in this land."

Walter's dark eyes glance around the crowd. He sees his Grandma's kind face. She smiles at him. Walter puts his shoulders back. He makes himself look as tall as he can.

Walter speaks again. "Then about 500 years ago, many new people came from across the sea." The drum music stops. Now a new group of students walk to the front. Some are dressed like the **explorers**. Some carry fishing nets. Some carry furs. They are the fur traders.

"The visitors came from Europe," explains Walter. "Their ways were very different from our ways. Our people had respect for nature. They killed only the animals they needed for their own use. The **newcomers** did not want animals just for food and clothing. They wanted lots of animal furs. They wanted to sell these furs to make money."

1. How would you have felt if you had been one of the Native people meeting the Europeans for the first time? How would you have felt if you had been one of the Europeans meeting the Native people?

The students act out what happened when the newcomers met the **Native** peoples. The two groups pretend to trade. The group of strangers take furs from the group dressed as Native people. In trade, the new people give iron tools and metal pots for cooking. They give the Native people guns and bright glass beads.

"Soon the newcomers also asked the Natives to help them explore the land," says Walter.

The children on stage show how this took place.

"Our people guided the newcomers through the forests of what is now Canada," Walter says. "They taught the newcomers how to make canoes. They taught them how to make snowshoes."

"When the visitors were hungry, our people helped them find wild **game**. They showed them which wild roots and berries were good to eat.

"Our people taught the newcomers a lot about living with nature," says Walter. "They taught them to be resourceful. They did this because they believed in the Great Spirit. They believed the Great Spirit wanted them to **co-operate** with the strangers from across the sea."

"Our people and the newcomers shared with each other what they knew. They learned many things from each other," says Walter. "But they all had some problems."

On stage, several children start to fight. Walter explains. "Some tribes fought with each other over furs. They all wanted furs to trade with the newcomers."

"Different groups of newcomers fought with each other too," says Walter. "The English often fought with the French. Often our people were drawn into the wars."

On stage, some students now slump down. They look ill.

"Another problem was that our people got some diseases from the newcomers. Our people had never had diseases such as measles and **smallpox**. Their bodies were not used to fighting these diseases. Many of our people died."

What Happened to the Land

Sad music plays. After a few moments, another group of students comes on stage.

These students play the part of the **settlers** from Europe. Some carry axes. They pretend to chop down trees and clear land. Some pretend to build log cabins.

"The settlers were different from the fur traders," Walter explains. "They were also different from the explorers. The settlers did not just want to trade and explore. They wanted to stay and live off the land. They wanted to build lasting homes for themselves. To do this, they felt they needed land—lots of it."

Two more students now come on stage. They play the part of government leaders. They carry papers in their hands. These papers are **treaties**, or agreements about land.

1. How did the arrival of the newcomers affect the Native people?

2. Describe in your own words some differences between the Native people and the Europeans.

This is the way a Canadian artist imagined the scene of a Native chief meeting an early explorer. The explorer is Jacques Cartier.

On stage, the students show what happened. The Native leaders and the government leaders sit down with each other. They begin to talk. The talk goes on and on. At last, both groups sign the treaties.

"Our leaders and the government leaders did not understand the treaties in the same way," says Walter. "Our leaders thought that they were just agreeing to share the land with the settlers. To our people, land was like air to breathe. It was not something that could be bought and sold. They did not mean to sell it. However, government leaders thought the Native people sold the land to the settlers."

Walter explains what happened next while the students act it out. "More and more settlers came from Europe. They

An early settler family built a small log shelter for their first home. This family settled in Southern Ontario.

planted crops on the land. They built fences around their crops. They built towns and cities. As time went on, the settlers took up more and more of the land.

"Some areas of land, however, were set aside for our people. In time, many of our people began to live only in those areas. Our people felt sad about this, but it was hard for them to stand up for what they wanted. By this time, more settlers than Native people lived in this land.

The drum music plays again. On stage, the students start to dance. Walter's teacher walks to the front. She speaks to the audience. "This is the end of our play," she says.

"You have seen many of the things that happened through the years. The story does not end here. In the last few years, new things have been happening. Next year, we will have a play to tell that part of the story."

Slowly the curtain closes. The people in the crowd clap.

Visiting Bev and Aunt Rose

It is summer, and school is over. The days are hot and bright.

Each summer, Native people all over Canada gather for pow-wow dancing. The pow-wow at "Indian Days" in Winnipeg is one of the biggest ones in the country. Many people come.

Walter and Grandma fly to Winnipeg to visit Aunt Rose and Bev. They want to dance in the pow-wow at Indian Days.

Walter and the others leave Aunt Rose's house. They take the bus to the Indian Days celebrations. Bev and Aunt Rose lead the way across the grass to the pow-wow circle. Walter and Grandma follow.

They hear the pounding of the pow-wow drum. They hear the rattle of beads and shells. They see the dancers jump and whirl to the music.

Walter and Bev feel excited. They are ready to dance. They are wearing their dance costumes.

Bev wears a dress with long **fringes**. She has a beaded headband. Red and yellow feathers stick up from the back of her headband.

Walter wears his moose-hide shirt and leggings. His belt is covered with bright beads. He has beaded armbands and leg bands. On his head, Walter wears a headpiece of deer hair. This kind of headpiece is called a **roach**.

Now the singers are starting a new song. The song is a special one for children. It is called the "Hoot Owl" song.

Bev and Walter step into the ring of dancers. They twirl and dance to the drum beats. Bev's fringes and feathers bounce with the music. She feels good. She feels proud to be an Indian. She is glad to be dancing with the other Native dancers. They all seem like brothers and sisters to her.

The voices of the singers sound high and sweet. They sing about the hoot owl. Then they sing about a **spirit helper** who came to help a young boy, long ago.

When the "Hoot Owl" song is done, another dance starts. It is the Snake Dance. Grandma and Aunt Rose join in.

After the Snake Dance comes the Buffalo Dance. It makes the dancers think of days gone by. In those days, the people hunted buffalo all across the plains.

Bannock Burgers

By the time the Buffalo Dance is over, Bev and Walter are hungry. "Let's go get bannock burgers," says Bev. Grandma goes with them. Aunt Rose stays in the dance ring with some of her friends. Walter and Grandma sit down in the shade of a tree. Bev goes to buy the burgers. They are made of meat and a chewy kind of bread called **bannock**.

Walter, Bev, and Grandma sit quietly in the shade to eat. From the pow-wow ring comes the pounding of the drum. The high voices of the singers float on the summer air.

Making Bannock

Bannock is a bread the Native people started making many years ago, soon after they first got flour from the Europeans. The Native people traded animal furs for the flour. Here is a recipe for bannock.

Ingredients

500 mL flour
2.5 mL salt
15 mL baking powder
250 mL water or milk
30 mL cooking oil or soft lard

Directions

1. Mix the flour, salt, and baking powder in a large bowl. Stir them well with a wooden spoon.

2. Add the oil or lard and the milk or water to the dry ingredients. Stir well.

3. When the dough becomes too stiff to stir, mix it with your hands. Sprinkle a bit of flour on the counter. Put the dough on the counter and knead with your fists till the dough is smooth.

4. Shape the dough into a flat round cake about three centimetres thick. Prick it with a fork about 25 times.

5. Preheat the oven to 165°C. Bake the bannock for 20 minutes. It will be golden brown when it is done.

6. Eat the bannock warm, with butter and jam or honey.

Stick Bannock

If your family goes camping, or if you have a picnic where you can have a fire, you can make bannock over a fire. Use the same recipe and follow these instructions.

1. Roll the dough into a long rope. Each person can use enough dough for a serving.

2. Wind the rope around a stick.

3. Hold the stick over the coals of the fire. Turn the stick often so the dough will bake on all sides.

4. The stick bannock is ready to eat when the dough is no longer sticky on the inside, and the outside is crusty and brown.

The Friendship Centre

The next day Bev and Aunt Rose take Walter and Grandma to see the **Friendship Centre**. The Native People's Friendship Centre is near downtown Winnipeg. It is a good place to meet and relax with other Native people. You can play checkers, find out how to get a job, or get help with finding a place to stay. Walter and Bev play ping pong while Aunt Rose and Grandma have tea with some other people.

Then Grandma finds an old game on a shelf. The game is called Ring and Pin. Grandma, Walter, and Bev take turns playing.

"This was a good game for our hunters, long ago," says Grandma. "It taught them to be quick with their hands and eyes."

Walter learns that the Friendship Centre is not just a place for games. It is also a place where Native people can meet to talk. At the Friendship Centre, they can share news. They can work together to solve their problems.

"To me, a Friendship Centre seems like a bridge," says Aunt Rose.

Walter laughs. "That sounds strange. It's just a big building to me."

"Turn around, Walter." Aunt Rose points to the wall. "Look at all those pictures. Maybe they'll help show you what I mean. See, the pictures are in two groups."

The pictures were drawn by Native children in Winnipeg schools. One group of pictures shows life on a reserve. The other group shows life in a big city.

"See what big differences there are," says Aunt Rose. "The homes in the city look different from the ones on the reserve. In the city, many people live in apartments."

Aunt Rose goes on. "See the jobs people are doing in the city. They are different from the ones on the reserve. On the reserve, we live with nature because we still hunt and fish and trap. In the city, people work in big stores and offices. It is hard to get used to such big changes. Friendship Centres are like bridges between reserve life and city life. They can help people find places to live. They can help them find jobs. You see what I mean, Walter?"

"Hey!" says Walter. "Maybe we can put that in our next school play. The teacher told our class to think of ideas for it."

A Visit with Chief Tom Wood

Just then a tall man with grey hair walks in.

"Hello, Tom," says Grandma. "I was hoping I'd get to see you."

Grandma introduces him to the others. He is Chief Tom Wood, an old friend. Chief Wood was chosen to help organize meetings with Native leaders and the government. He works hard to help make Native peoples' lives better all over Canada.

Chief Wood sits down. Aunt Rose pours some tea for him.

Walter pulls his chair closer. "Did you go to the pow-wow?" Walter asks.

"Yes, I did," says Chief Wood. "I was glad to see so many people there enjoying themselves."

"I think our people feel more sure of themselves than they used to," Grandma tells him.

"Yes, I think you're right," Chief Wood nods. "We will always have problems. The good part is that we aren't so afraid to talk to the government any more. When the White Paper came out, we gave the government a good reply."

"What's the White Paper?" Walter asks.

"The White Paper was written by the government of Canada," Chief Wood answers. "It said Native people have no special rights. It said they should be treated just like everyone else in Canada."

"Well, isn't that right?" asks Bev. "Shouldn't we be treated like everyone else?"

"No, not really Bev," he says. "Just think about it. We're not the same as other Canadians, are we? This land was the home of our people for hundreds of years before the Europeans came. We belong to this land. Through the treaties, we gave up many rights. We gave up big parts of the land as well. In return, the government made us promises.

"They said we would have certain rights. For instance, we have special rights to hunt and fish. We have a right to an education in our own schools. We have a right to be paid for the use of our land. We can't just forget about things like that now."

"I didn't know about all this," says Bev.

Chief Wood goes on. "I and the other chiefs did not like the White Paper at all. We wrote down our ideas about it. In 1970 we all went to Ottawa. We gave the government our paper called *Citizens Plus*. Some people call it the Red Paper."

"Then what happened?" asks Walter.

Some of the Native leaders met in Ottawa with government leaders in 1970. The Prime Minister at the time was Pierre Trudeau.

"Many Canadians began to understand us, maybe for the first time. They began to see how we belong in this country like nobody else does. The Canadian people began objecting to the way the government was treating us. The government began to listen."

"That's good, isn't it?" says Bev.

"Yes, very good," says Chief Wood. "But we still have a long way to go."

Chief Wood goes on. "There are still a lot of problems in the North. Big companies are mining up there. They're drilling for oil.

"**Inuit** leaders say the land is theirs. They say no one should mine or drill without asking. They say the non-Native people do not respect nature. They spoil the hunting and fishing."

Aunt Rose sighs. "How can problems like that ever be solved?"

"It's not easy," says Chief Wood. "But at least the Inuit and the government people are talking to each other. They have already made some agreements about land."

"What about the way things are run on the reserves?" asks Aunt Rose. "I think we should have more say about that."

"Yes," nods Chief Wood, "I agree. I think the government of Canada has too much to say about the reserves now."

"I saw something about that on TV," adds Walter. "Weren't there some meetings about it?"

"That's right," says Chief Wood. "In 1981 we formed a new group. We call it the Assembly of First Nations. It speaks for all Native peoples on the reserves. In March 1984 we met with government leaders from across Canada. We talked about a plan for Native self-government."

"But we and the government didn't agree," Grandma adds.

"No, not yet," says Chief Wood. "We are still working on it."

Chief Wood stands up. "I must be off now. You kids take care. Exciting things could happen in years to come. Maybe you two will help make them happen."

Walter laughs. "Last year our school put on a play about the history of our people. In the fall we're going to have another play about what happened next. Do you think you could come, Chief Wood?"

"Say, I'd like that." Chief Wood smiles.

"We'll write and tell you when the play is," Walter says.

"You do that," Chief Wood replies. Then he waves and goes out the door.

Native Peoples Long Ago

Introduction

Sometimes when Walter was getting ready for the play, he tried to imagine what life was like long ago. He wished he could go back in time and look over the whole country of what is now Canada. What if Walter *could* go back in time before explorers came from Europe? What if you could go back in time? What would you see?

You would see a great land stretching from sea to sea. You would see only plains, mountains, lakes, rivers, and streams. In those days there were no highways. There were no smokestacks or TV towers. There were no fur **trading posts** or railway tracks or pipelines. There were no big cities.

In the forests and plains and mountains lived the Native peoples of this land. They lived in all the different parts of what we now call Canada. How they lived depended on the part of the country they lived in and the kinds of plants and animals there.

Walter's **ancestors** were Woodland Cree Indians. There were many other groups of Native peoples. The different groups are shown on the chart. What can you learn from the pictures about each group? Use the map on page 28 to find out where each group lived. Then read the next section of the book to find out more about how the different groups lived.

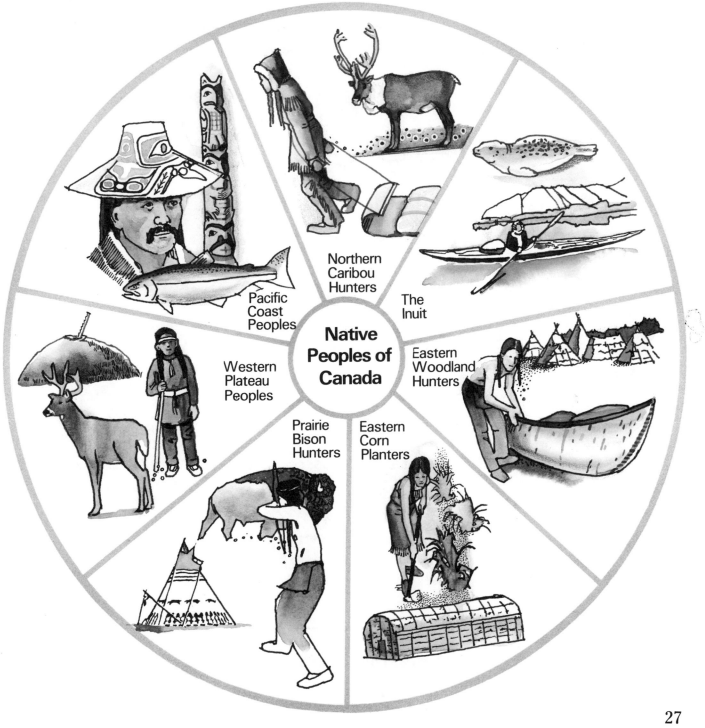

Northern
Caribou
Hunters

Pacific
Coast
Peoples

The
Inuit

Native
Peoples of
Canada

Western
Plateau
Peoples

Eastern
Woodland
Hunters

Prairie
Bison
Hunters

Eastern
Corn
Planters

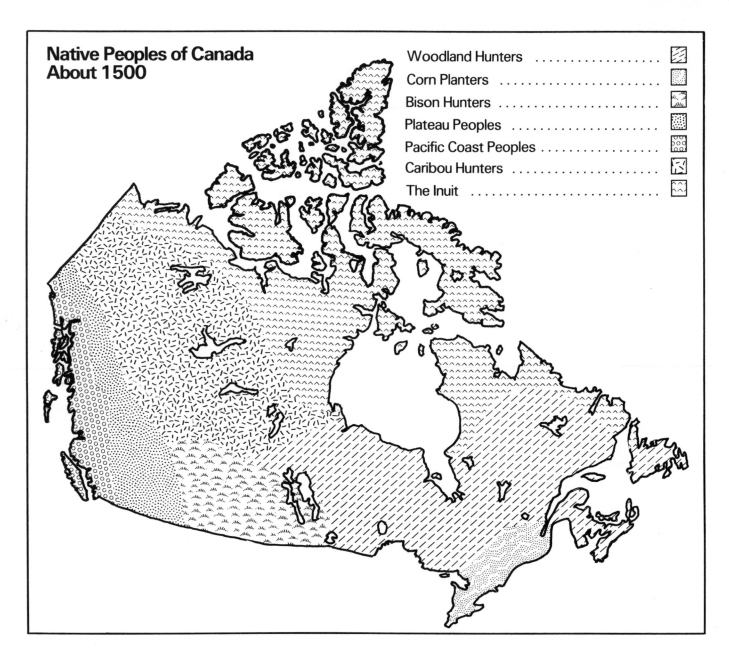

Native Peoples of Canada About 1500

Woodland Hunters . . . .
Corn Planters . . . .
Bison Hunters . . . .
Plateau Peoples . . . .
Pacific Coast Peoples . . . .
Caribou Hunters . . . .
The Inuit . . . .

Use an atlas to find a map of Canada. Find where you live on the map. Then find the same area on the map above. Which group of Native peoples lived in the area where you live now?

28

Eastern Woodland Hunters

For thousands of years, people lived in the Eastern Woodlands of our country. The Native People who first lived there are now known as the Eastern Woodland Hunters. They hunted forest animals, large and small. They picked wild berries. They caught fish in the many lakes and rivers and streams.

It was not always easy for the Woodland Hunters to find food. They had to know where to look for it. They moved from place to place. Wherever the hunting or berry-picking or fishing was good—that is where they went.

The land of the Woodland Hunters was rugged, with many rocks and trees. In the north were spruce trees and huge **swamps**. The Native people called these wet areas **muskeg.**

Farther south grew birch trees, with their useful white bark. Pines also grew there. There were tall elms and sugar maples. All over the Woodland Hunters' homeland were rivers, lakes, and streams.

Lone Bird was an Eastern Woodland child. When she was a baby, her mother wrapped her snugly and laced her to a wooden cradle board. Her mother carried the cradle board on her back. That way, Lone Bird was always close to her mother.

As soon as Lone Bird took her first steps, she learned to share in her family's work. At first she helped by finding little sticks for the fire. Later, Lone Bird learned to bring fresh water to camp. Her brother, Young Bear, helped too.

Algonkian Words

Most Eastern Woodland Hunters spoke Algonkian (al-gonk'-i-an) languages. About 200 Algonkian words have been taken into English. Here are a few of the most common ones.

moose	Ottawa	moccasin
skunk	toboggan	muskeg
raccoon	wigwam	
chipmunk	tomahawk	

Some of these words are used in French as well as in English.

The two of them carried the water from a nearby river or stream.

When Lone Bird grew a bit older, she learned to guide a **birchbark** canoe through the water. This was sometimes hard work. There were rocks and **rapids** to watch for.

Young Bear learned to break a trail. He walked ahead of his family group, finding a way through the woods. In the winter the whole family walked on snowshoes. They loaded their things onto toboggans, which they dragged along through the snowy forest.

Lone Bird and Young Bear and their parents lived in a **wigwam**. This kind of home was light. It was easy to carry.

Summer Gatherings

Lone Bird and Young Bear liked the summers because of the great summer gatherings. Large numbers of their people camped together. They camped in an area where there was lots of food.

Sometimes this area was a part of the woods where deer-hunting was good. Sometimes the area was near a spot where fish were spawning. Other times, it was a place where lots of berries or wild rice grew.

The children had a good time at the summer feasts. They laughed and talked with their friends. They danced to the music of drums and rattles. Sometimes they took part in sports. **Wrestling** was one of these. Shooting with bows and arrows was another.

Often Lone Bird and Young Bear listened to the older people tell stories. The children liked listening to stories. Stories were important because the Native people did not have a written language. The older people told stories to the young people and children. When the children grew up, they told the same stories to their children.

1. Make a list of the kinds of trees that grew in the area where Lone Bird and Little Bear lived. In what ways were these trees useful to the children's family?

2. How did the Woodland Hunters' homes suit their style of life?

Telling the stories over and over meant that they would not be forgotten. Sometimes there were other things that Lone Bird and Young Bear's people wanted to remember.

They recorded important things by drawing pictures. They drew on birchbark and rocks. That is how they recorded important dreams, songs, and the laws of their people.

In the summertime, Lone Bird and Young Bear joined with everyone else to get ready for winter. Warm winter clothes had to be made. Tools had to be repaired. Sometimes new tools or toboggans had to be made.

Wintertime

Usually, Lone Bird and Young Bear did not see many other children during the winter. Each family stayed in its own hunting area. There was not enough food in one area for large numbers of people. The children's father was a good hunter. He was good at hunting moose, deer, caribou, and bear. He was careful not to hunt all the animals in the area.

One year, during the summer gathering, he reported to the other hunters that the animals in his area were becoming too **scarce**. The next winter the family camped with another family where the animals were plentiful. The families were all used to sharing what they had.

Young Bear helped his father with the hunting. Lone Bird helped her mother do the cooking and sewing. She also helped her mother **snare** small **game**. In winter they all needed lots of warm clothes. Lone Bird and her mother kept their winter clothes well mended. On very cold days, Lone Bird and Young Bear wore underclothes made of soft, fluffy rabbit fur.

After the long, hard winter, everyone was eager for spring. Lone Bird and Young Bear watched for the birds to return. They listened for the frogs. They felt the changes in the air. They knew that after spring came summer, the time for feasting and fun.

Storytelling

Storytelling was a way the older people taught the children. Some stories told about what happened in the past. Other stories were lessons on how to get along with others. Some stories told about the plants and animals. Sometimes the stories taught what the people believed about the Great Spirit.

1. Why were the hunters of the Eastern Woodlands careful not to hunt all the animals in one area? What might have happened if the hunters had not been aware of the animals that were left?

2. Why did the Woodland Hunter families move around a lot?

Picture Writing

Long ago the Woodland Hunters used their language only for speaking. They wrote by drawing pictures. They drew on birchbark. Sometimes they drew on rocks and cliffs. Native picture writing can still be seen today, especially on the rocks and cliffs around the Great Lakes.

Sometimes the Woodland Hunters used their pictures to record important laws or dreams. Sometimes they used the pictures to send messages.

The Woodland Hunters used a reddish colouring material. It is called **red ochre**. It is a kind of earth.

Here are samples of pictures that the Woodland Hunters used in their writing. Try to guess what each picture means. The answers are at the bottom of the page.

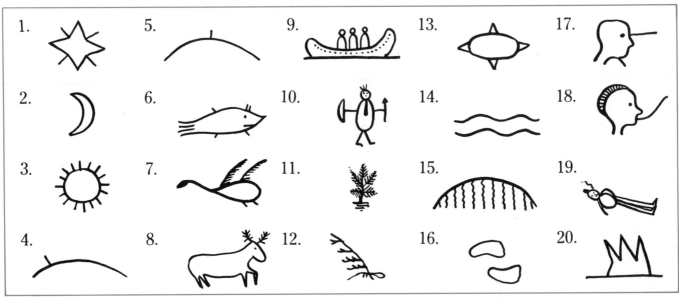

1. star	5. noon	9. canoe	13. Great Spirit	17. see
2. moon	6. fish	10. war	14. river, stream	18. speak
3. sun	7. water bird	11. tree	15. rain, cloudy	19. dream
4. sunrise	8. deer, moose	12. old tree	16. come	20. mountains

Eastern Corn Planters

Here is a **legend** about how one of the main groups of Native peoples became farmers. Many of the Native peoples used legends to explain their history.

Once a great hunter was on a journey. After a long day, he went to sleep by his fire. Suddenly he woke. A woman was standing near the fire. "The Great Spirit has sent me to marry you," she said.

The hunter had never seen the woman before, but he agreed right away. "We will do as the Great Spirit wishes," he said.

The hunter spent a happy winter with his new wife. In the spring he took her back to his people.

Now, the hunter's people had always found their food by hunting and fishing. They did now know about farming.

The Great Spirit had given corn seeds to the hunter's wife. She gave them to the people. "Let us dig beds in the earth for the seed to lie in," she told them. "Let us cover the seeds softly, and watch over them. By and by they will come to life."

Sure enough, that's what happened. Tiny green plants began to grow in the sunshine. They looked like a strange kind of grass. As the plants grew, they formed long green "ears." Inside these ears grew plump yellow cobs of corn!

The group of people in this story became known as the Eastern Corn Planters. Because they grew some of their

Corn

The corn that the women grew gave them more than food. They used the leaves for weaving mats and slippers. The women also used the leaves as a wrapping for corn cakes being cooked in the fire. The dry cornstalks were sometimes used to make dolls and other toys. After the corn kernels were taken off the cobs, the cobs were used for scrub brushes. The women made necklaces from dried corn kernels. Dried corn kernels were also good for making rattles.

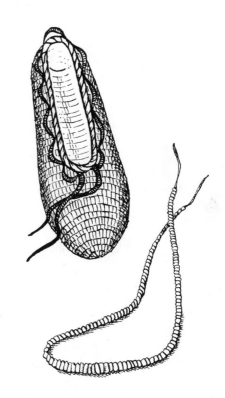

35

food, they did not need to move around to go hunting. They built their villages in forest clearings. Often they lived in these villages for years.

Black Lynx was the name of a boy who lived in one of these villages. He did not live in a wigwam as Lone Bird and Young Bear did. He lived in a **longhouse**.

Black Lynx's father and the other men built the longhouse. The frame was made of poles from trees. The men made shingles of bark from elm trees. They used these elm shingles to cover the pole frame.

There were 24 families in the longhouse where Black Lynx lived. Each family had its own section. There was a row of fire pits down the middle. Black Lynx and his family shared their fire pit with another family.

Black Lynx's village was surrounded by rolling hills. Rivers and streams flowed through the woodlands. Close to the village were big fields of corn. Each spring, Black Lynx's mother and the other women planted the corn. During the summer they hoed the fields with hoes made of deer shoulder blades. The long warm summers were just right for growing corn.

Black Lynx and his friends loved to play in the hills around the village. They practised hunting with their bows and arrows. They wanted to become good hunters and hunt deer with the men.

Black Lynx also liked to climb trees. His favourite game was to find the tallest tree and climb to the top. He liked to look out over the whole countryside.

One day Black Lynx was sitting outside the longhouse with his grandmother. She was making buckskin clothes for the family. She had just made a buckskin dress for Black Lynx's mother. Now she was making a jacket and leggings for Black Lynx.

As Grandmother worked, she told Black Lynx stories.

Beans and Squash

Beans and squash, as well as corn, were important crops for Black Lynx's village. The women made baskets for their seeds. Each basket had three different sections. That way the women could carry their three different kinds of seeds without getting them mixed up. The women planted the corn in little mounds of loose soil. They planted a bean beside each corn plant. The corn stalk made a sturdy pole for the bean vine to climb. The squash plant spread between the corn and bean mounds.

1. Look at the map on page 28. In what part of the country did the Corn Planters live? Which word describes the area best: northwestern, northeastern, southwestern, southeastern?

2. Why could the Corn Planters live in the same village for many years?

The Corn Planters had another use for wampum, besides trading. They strung the shells in certain patterns to record important decisions the leaders made. Someone in the village then kept the band of wampum in a safe place.

Here is one story that she told. It explains some of the Corn Planters' beliefs about nature and the world around them.

Corn, beans, and squash are three sisters. They are daughters of mother earth. Since they are sisters, they like to be planted together. In late summer, when the crops are ripe, we hold **festivals**. We give thanks to the spirits of the three sisters—corn, beans, and squash. They provide us with food.

Trade and Travel

The Corn Planters were not only farmers. They were also hunters and fishermen. They were traders, too. Black Lynx's father often went away on trading trips. He and the other men traded cornmeal, beans, **herbs**, and other things from their fields. In return, they got things they needed from the Woodland Hunters. Some of these were: animal skins, dried meat, and boxes made out of birchbark.

The Corn Planters also traded their goods for birchbark canoes. Their homeland had few birch trees large enough to make good canoes. This is why they had to trade for canoes. Canoes were important for summer travel. During the winter, Black Lynx's family travelled mostly on snowshoes.

Sometimes Black Lynx's father and the other men used a form of money in their trading. One name for their money was *wampumpeak*. It means "a string of white beads." **Wampum** is the shortened form. Wampum was made from special clam shells. Some of the shells were white and others were purple.

Black Lynx was glad to see his father when he came back from a trading trip. He often brought a special gift for Black Lynx.

Often the men returned from summer trading just in time for the great Harvest Festival. The women and children had harvested the corn, beans, squash, and other crops. They had stored them safely in the longhouses. It was time for Black Lynx's people to thank the Great Spirit for his good gifts from the fields.

1. Tell in your own words what both Black Lynx and Lone Bird might do on a nice summer day.

2. Why do you think the Corn Planters became traders?

Visiting a Longhouse

What do you think it would be like to visit Black Lynx's longhouse? Let's imagine what it would be like.

We go in through a door at one end of the building. The door is made of elm bark. If it were winter, an animal skin would hang over the doorway.

Inside the longhouse, the light is dim. It takes our eyes a few moments to get used to it. We pass through a storage area. Here the wood is piled up to be used for the fires.

Now we go through a second doorway into a big room. The room is very long. Down through the middle is a section about three metres wide. In the middle is a row of twelve fire pits. Opposite each fire pit, along each wall, are separate sections. Each section has a huge platform built against the wall.

One family uses each section. At night they sleep on the platform. During the day they can use it for a place to sit. Above the platform in each section is a shelf. Each family uses this shelf for storage. They keep things like snowshoes, baskets, and pots there.

Now we look up high towards the roof. Bunches of dried corncobs are hanging from the rafters. There are also dried herbs. At one end, we see smoked deer meat hanging from the rafters. The people store much of their food this way.

The Pound

This diagram shows the shape of the pound.

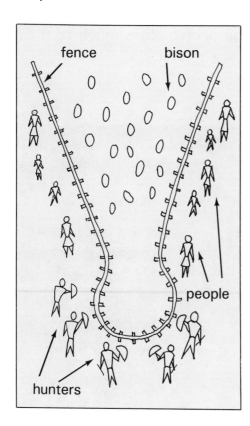

1. What did the people do to prepare for a bison hunt?

2. Why was it so important that everyone co-operate during a bison hunt? What might have happened if the people had not worked together?

Prairie Bison Hunters

Long ago a group of Native people lived on the windy western plains of what is now Canada. Their land was one of wide open spaces. Few trees grew, except in the river valleys. Summers were hot. Winters were often bitterly cold.

The people who lived on the plains are called the Prairie Bison Hunters. The **bison**, or the shaggy brown buffalo, was very important to them. They hunted the bison for food. Its hide gave the people blankets. The other parts of the bison gave many of the things the people needed. The bison hunt was the centre of their life.

Spotted Calf was a young girl who lived on the plains long before any settlers came to this land. Her family and the others in her tribe moved wherever the **herds** of bison went.

To get ready for the hunt, the people sang special songs. Spotted Calf's father and the other hunters spread herbs on themselves. They believed the herbs would bring success. The hunters followed the rules they had made for working together on a hunt. If a hunter went off on his own, he would be punished. He might frighten away the herd. A herd of bison was much too big for a hunter to hunt alone.

Everyone in Spotted Calf's tribe helped get ready for the hunt—all the men, women, and children. They chopped down trees to use for building a fence. In this way the people made a large **corral** or **pound**. Spotted Calf and the other children helped by carrying branches.

Once the pound was built, the hunt started. Spotted Calf's older brother and the other **scouts** brought the herd of

The Travois

The *travois* was made of wood and had a small platform where the load would be tied. A *travois* had no wheels. It was dragged along the ground.

bison toward the corral. To do this, the scouts put on wolf skins. Then the scouts crawled on their hands and knees. The bison kept moving to get away from the "wolves."

The bison herd moved into the wide end of the pound. Then Spotted Calf and her mother, along with the other women and children, helped to frighten the herd along. They shouted and waved blankets. They darted out at the animals. This made the bison nervous. The bison galloped farther and farther into the fenced area. At last they were trapped in the small round area of the pound. There Spotted Calf's father and the other hunters killed the bison with their arrows and spears.

Preparing the Meat

After the hunters made the kill, the women had lots of work to do. They all helped to skin the bison. They cut up the meat. Then they loaded it onto V-shaped wooden **travois**. The dogs dragged these back to camp. In those days, dogs and *travois* were the only way that the Bison Hunters had to carry heavy loads. They themselves usually travelled on foot in summer.

Spotted Calf and the other children ran behind the *travois*, laughing and shouting. The bison hunt was exciting for them. They were happy that many bison had been killed. Now their people would have lots to eat. Everyone enjoyed a big feast.

After the feast the women dried some of the meat. They sliced the meat very thin and hung it on racks to dry in the sun. The meat was good to eat dried. The women also made **pemmican** from some of the dried meat.

Pemmican is a food that will keep for years. It is a mixture of dried meat and fat. Sometimes berries are added.

Spotted Calf and the other girls worked with their mothers. They each dried some bison meat of their own. The girls made their own pemmican. Then they stored it in bags made of animal skin.

Spotted Calf had a number of these bags. They all contained food that she had dried herself. Some bags held dried deer and moose meat. In other bags were dried berries, wild cherries, wild turnips, and other roots.

"You can do the cooking today," Spotted Calf's mother sometimes told her. Her mother might say this if she was busy making clothes for the family. The family needed a lot of clothes for the cold prairie winter. Father and the boys needed shirts and leggings. Mother and the girls needed dresses and leggings. Everybody had to have moccasins. All these things were made from animal skins—often deer or elk hides.

Spotted Calf might not feel much like cooking sometimes, but she always did it. She knew that in a family each

Tools

The Bison Hunter people made all their tools. The women used knives made of stone or bone to cut up the meat. They used scrapers for scraping the insides of animal skins clean. The scrapers were also made of stone or bone.

1. What part of your life would you enjoy most if you were a child in a Bison Hunter family?

person's help was needed. She made a good meal for her parents and brothers and sisters.

The family ate outdoors near their bison-skin **tipi**. After the meal, Spotted Calf and her younger brother, Star Wolf, were ready to play.

One day Spotted Calf and Star Wolf ran beyond the camp circle of tipis. They went to play in a clump of willows and bushes on the edge of a little lake. Other children were there, too. Star Wolf ran on ahead to join them.

As Spotted Calf walked toward the lake, she saw a group of men on the horizon. She was afraid that enemy warriors were coming. She wanted to warn Star Wolf and the others. She did not want the enemy to notice her. What could she do? She hid in some tall weeds. She cried out like a wounded **hare**. Spotted Calf waited a moment. Then she cried again.

Star Wolf and the others heard her. Right away, they left the lake. Quickly they sneaked through the tall grass into the camp circle. There they were safe.

Spotted Calf was glad they had agreed on a signal so they could warn each other of danger. The children copied different sounds of animals and birds. Each sound had a special meaning.

After a while Spotted Calf and Star Wolf wanted to go back to the lake to play. Their father would not let them. "It's not safe for you to go outside the camp any more today," he said.

Spotted Calf was angry. She started to talk back.

Her grandfather stopped her. "Your father is right," he said. "Come here and sit by me. Star Wolf, you come too. I will tell you a story." The children sat with their grandfather. They knew they would have to wait for another day to play outside the circle of tipis. Spotted Calf and Star Wolf curled up on a bison-hide rug and listened to Grandfather's story.

The Circle

The circle shape was important to the Bison Hunter people. They lived on the flat prairie. They could see the sky all around them. The world looked like a big circle where the sky and land came together. The sun also looked like a great circle in the sky.

The Bison Hunters lived in tipis. These tents had pole frames covered with bison hides. The hides were sewn together with bison **sinew**. Each tipi was shaped like a cone. This meant that the bottom rim formed a circle. When the people made camp, they set their tipis in a large circle.

The circle was important because it was a sign of the Great Spirit. The Bison Hunter people believed the Great Spirit of the sun ruled over all.

The Bison

The bison was like a walking department store. From this one animal the Prairie Bison Hunters got almost everything they needed.

From this part of the bison . . .	they got this.
meat	food for themselves and their dogs
hide	clothing, blankets, tipi coverings, war shields, saddles, bridles, thongs, tub-like boats for crossing rivers
horns	spoons, cups, weapon points, tools of various kinds
bones	scrapers and other tools
brains	used in tanning hides
sinew	thread for sewing
feet and hoofs	glue to attach arrowheads to shafts
hair	halters, ropes
stomach	could be used as a cooking pot if necessary
dry dung	fuel to make fires for cooking
tail	fly swatter

Western Plateau Peoples

Suppose you could choose to live in your favourite kind of **landscape**. What would you choose? Would you like to live in a hot dry area like a desert? There you could smell sagebrush and see a cactus blooming.

Would you rather live in a green forest? What about grasslands or mountain slopes?

All these different kinds of landscapes are found on the inland plateau of what is now British Columbia. This plateau was the homeland of Native peoples long ago. We call the many groups who lived there the Western Plateau Peoples.

If you could have visited these people, you might have met a boy named Broken Arrow.

Broken Arrow lived in an unusual house. It was built partly under ground. From the outside it looked like a mound of earth and branches. The doorway was a hole in the centre of the roof. Broken Arrow went into his house by using a notched, slanted pole like a ladder. When he wanted to go into the house, he would call out to warn his mother. She might be cooking over the fire beneath the doorway. This gave her a chance to cover the cooking pots so that no dirt would fall into the food.

Broken Arrow's winter home was warm and cozy. In the summer his family lived in a cone-shaped tent.

Broken Arrow's people had many different sources of food. In the grasslands the people hunted **antelope**. In the forests they trapped deer, **elk**, and woodland **caribou**. Sometimes they trapped bear, **cougar**, and **lynx**.

The Plateau People hunted mountain goats. In the rivers salmon were plentiful. Wherever the Plateau People found wild berries, they picked them. They dug up tasty wild roots. With bows and arrows they shot birds.

Broken Arrow and his sister, Lily Flower, helped to find food for the family. Lily Flower and her friends often dug up the roots of flowering plants called **camas**. On the hillsides where the camas grew, the ground was often hard. The girls had to use sharp digging sticks made of tough wood. It was hard work!

A Plateau

A **plateau** is a high area of land. British Columbia's inland plateau lies between two large mountain ranges. To the east are the Rocky Mountains. The Coast Range is to the west. The plateau is very large —about 1450 kilometres north and south, and 250 to 300 kilometres east and west. Use an atlas to find this plateau on a map of Canada.

1. What did Lily Flower do to help find food for her family?

51

When their skin bags were full of roots, the girls took them home. Like all the Plateau Peoples, they usually walked wherever they went. They carried their loads on their backs. If they had dogs, the people put backpacks on the backs of the dogs.

Back at camp, Lily Flower and her friends were not allowed to bake the roots that they had dug. That was work for their grandmothers. Only the old women knew how to do it just right. When the camas roots were done, they looked black and sticky. They tasted good.

Broken Arrow loved the baked camas roots. He took some with him when he went out to hunt deer. The young men often hunted deer by themselves.

Usually Broken Arrow wore a deerskin shirt, leggings, and moccasins. But for hunting deer, he put on a special outfit. He wore a deerskin coat with the fur left on. On his head he wore a hat made from a deer's head. As he crept through the forest, he looked like a deer.

After some time, Broken Arrow came to a pit that he had dug earlier. He had dug this pit along a deer trail and had covered it with leaves and branches. The deer could not see that it was a trap. Sure enough, when Broken Arrow got close, he found that a deer had fallen into his trap. Quickly he killed it with his spear.

Now Broken Arrow's family had fresh deer meat to eat. They would share the meat with others in the camp. Broken Arrow felt happy. He was only thirteen, but he had shown that he was a good hunter.

Broken Arrow never killed deer except when his family needed food. Like other Native peoples, Broken Arrow thought of the animals as gifts from nature. Nature gave the people their food and everything else they needed. When Broken Arrow was very young, he learned never to waste the good gifts of nature.

1. Tell in your own words how Broken Arrow showed that he had respect for nature.

2. What kind of clothing did Broken Arrow wear when he went deer hunting? Why did he wear those clothes?

3. Do you and your family use the "gifts of nature" as Broken Arrow and his family did? Where does your food come from?

A Shaped Poem

The Native poet wrote this poem about the life of the Plateau Peoples long ago. In what shape did he place the words? Why? How do you think the hunter felt?

Try writing a shaped poem. What have you learned about the Plateau Peoples? Write your poem about something in the life of Broken Arrow. Then write a shaped poem about something important in your own life. Perhaps you could paint pictures to go with your poems.

Hunter's Lament

goose goose goose

why fly so high ?   goose

goose

goose goose

goose

Edward John

Building a Mound House

Broken Arrow's mound house was a comfortable place to live in the winter. To build the house, first his father drove a stake in the ground in the middle of the area. He tied a line to the stake. Then he tied a stick to the end of the line. He drew a circle on the ground by walking around in a circle. He scratched the ground with the stick as he walked. Next came the big job—digging.

The whole family worked together to dig out the earth inside the circle. They used digging sticks to loosen the earth. Then they carried the earth in baskets and piled it beside the circle. When the hole was close to two metres deep, they put up a framework of logs. Over the logs smaller poles and brush were placed. Then over all the wood the people piled the earth they had dug. Their house was about six metres across. A hole about a metre and a half square at the top was the entrance. The hole was also the place for the smoke from the fire to escape.

Pacific Coast Peoples

Raven Hair was a girl who lived in a Pacific Coast village more than 500 years ago. The coastal **climate** was mild and moist. Summers were not too hot and winters were not too cold.

In the huge forests of cedar trees lived many wild animals. Mountain goats and bighorn sheep grazed on the mountain sides. In the coastal marshes grew ferns and lilies. The roots of these plants were good to eat. In the bays of the sea were all kinds of fish.

For Raven Hair and her people, spring was the best time of year. Thousands of salmon swam from the ocean into the rivers to spawn then. The people caught the salmon in fish traps behind rows of poles called **weirs**.

The first spring salmon that was taken from the trap was called the Salmon Prince. Raven Hair's people thought that this first fish was special. All the people in her village gathered on the riverbank to watch for the first fish to be caught.

Raven Hair had to stand on her toes so she could see through the crowd. As she watched, the elder lifted the Salmon Prince from the water. He laid the silver-red fish on a bed of ferns and water lilies.

Then the people of Raven Hair's village spoke to the Great Spirit. They thanked him for the first fish of the salmon harvest. They sang and prayed. They promised to take the salmon only for food. They vowed that they would never waste the Great Spirit's gifts.

1. Look at the map on page 28. Find the area where Raven Hair lived. Find out how far her area is from the part of the country where Lone Bird lived.

2. Why did Raven Hair's people think the first salmon of the spring catch was so special?

Salmon Weir

A weir was used to catch fish. The men gathered a lot of poles to make a fence across the shallow part of the river. They sharpened the ends of the poles and drove them into the bottom of the river. The women wove baskets from plant roots and reeds. The fish baskets were placed behind the fence. The rows of poles stopped the salmon as they swam up the river. The salmon looked for a way around the poles and swam into the baskets. Then the fish were trapped.

After this, the elder cut the salmon open. He cut it with a special white shell. As Raven Hair and the others watched, the elder carefully sliced the fish. Then he cooked it.

The people went to stand at the doors of their homes. Raven Hair's family and the other families from her house stood in front of their painted **cedar** house. There they waited for the young people of the village to bring them some of the salmon. Raven Hair felt proud. Her big brother Young Otter was helping.

Carefully, the young people took slices of salmon from the elder. They carried the fish to the waiting villagers. Each person got a small taste of the first spring salmon.

Why did Raven Hair's people treat the Salmon Prince with such care? They believed the salmon had a spirit. Like all Native peoples, the Pacific Coast groups believed fish, animals, birds, and plants all had spirits.

They believed that other natural things had spirits too. Water, for instance, had a spirit. Air had a spirit. So did rocks and mountains.

Raven Hair's people took great care with the gifts of nature. For instance, her father and the other men cut down trees to build their cedar houses. They would never cut down all the trees in a certain area.

They hunted animals for food, but they never killed more than they needed. In doing these things, Raven Hair's people were thinking of the future. They wanted to make sure the gifts of nature would always be there.

Trading and Giving Gifts

Raven Hair's people did not need to grow crops like Black Lynx's people, the Corn Planters. They did not need to be on the move like Spotted Calf's people, the Bison Hunters. Raven Hair's people had lots of food all around them. They only had to gather it.

The Pacific Coast groups did not travel far to get food. When they did travel, it was in order to trade with each other. One group traded copper up and down the coast. They travelled by cedar canoe.

Another group of Pacific Coast Peoples traded the oil of a fat little fish. This fish was called the **oolichan** or the candlefish. Still another group traded lovely blankets that they had woven. Sometimes they used mountain goats' wool to weave these blankets. Sometimes they used the wool of a special kind of small white dog.

All of Raven Hair's people made many beautiful things. They wove. They carved. They painted. They had time to do this work because they did not have to spend much time finding food. The climate was warm so the women did not have to spend much time making warm clothing.

Raven Hair and her grandmother could dig a big basket of clams and pick many berries and crab apples in one day. This food would last several days. They had time to work on the pretty mat that they were making. They wove it from cedar bark. They dyed the bark bright colours—orange from alder bark, and blue from berries.

Many of the things Raven Hair's people made were for gifts. Her people celebrated special events by having a **potlatch**. A potlatch is a feast. It was usually hosted by a wealthy chief. Raven Hair's grandfather, Grey Wolf, held a potlatch when her baby brother was born. There was a great feast. Grey Wolf gave many gifts to his guests from the neighbouring village.

People of the Cedar

Raven Hair's people lived a long time in one place. They built large, sturdy houses. They had good material for this. The men in Raven Hair's village built houses out of the wood of the red cedar tree. Cedar wood has a straight grain. It is not hard to split.

The house where Raven Hair lived was a bit like a Corn Planter longhouse. It was large enough for several families. Along the outside walls of the house stood several carved **totem poles**. The carvings on the poles were the faces of creatures. These faces showed the **clan** grouping, and the important animals or spirits who helped the clan. The totem poles were made of cedar, like the house.

The people in Raven Hair's village used the cedar tree in many ways. She and her grandmother used the bark to weave cloth for making clothes for the family. They made a long cedar bark dress for Raven Hair. The neck was trimmed with a strip of otter fur. The dress was nice to wear on cool days.

For Raven Hair's father and brothers, the women made cedar bark robes. They also made hats shaped like cones. These were good for the many rainy days on the Pacific Coast.

Raven Hair did not like to wear many clothes in the summer. Often she wore only a cedar bark apron. When the rain came pouring down, she sometimes wore one of the rain hats.

During the long rainy evenings, Raven Hair liked to play games. One of her favourite games was cat's cradle. She and her grandmother sometimes spent several hours making figures with string. Grandmother knew how to make many different animals. Raven Hair wanted to learn how to make all of them.

1. Why do you think Raven Hair's people are sometimes called "People of the Cedar"? Can you think of another name that would suit the Pacific Coast Peoples?

Clothing of the Pacific Coast Peoples

Most of the early Native peoples needed very warm clothing a lot of the time. However, on the West Coast the climate was warm. People needed fur clothing for only a few of the coldest days of the winter, and sometimes when it rained.

Raven Hair's family usually went barefoot. They made most of their clothes from cedar bark. They knew how to twist the bark into a thread that could be woven into a fairly soft

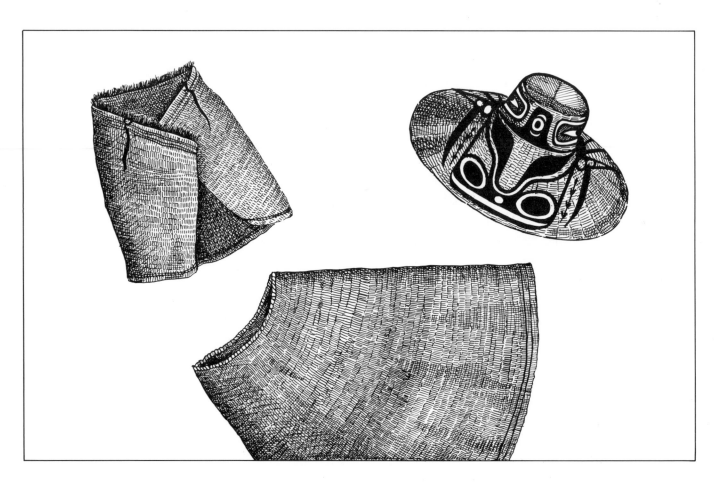

cloth. They wove their cloth on looms. The women made aprons for themselves to wear in warm weather. For cooler weather they wore cloaks or long dresses.

The men sometimes wore a cape around their shoulders. Often they slipped it around the waist when they were working.

Nearly everyone wore a hat. The hats were cone-shaped. They were made of strips of spruce root woven together. The hats protected the people from the hot sun in summer. The hats were very watertight, so that they were a good protection from the heavy winter rains.

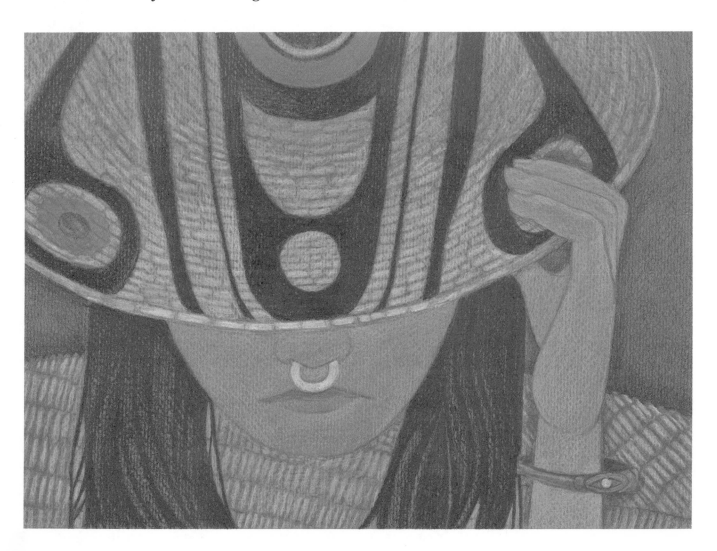

Northern Caribou Hunters

The boy was fifteen. His name was Brown Beaver. He had been alone in the woods for four days. All that time, he had eaten no food. He had had only water to drink. All he did was pray and wait. He was praying and waiting for a spirit helper. A spirit helper was a guardian spirit sent to help the person with his life.

At last Brown Beaver saw something. It was a spirit in the form of a moose. It was coming down from the sky.

"Don't be afraid," said the moose spirit kindly. "I have come to take care of you. I will be with you all your life. I will guard you against the evil spirits who haunt this land."

The guardian spirit gave Brown Beaver some food. Then he went back into the sky.

Long ago most Native people in what is now Canada believed in guardian spirits. The boy in the story belonged to the Native group we call the Caribou Hunters. What if we could visit Brown Beaver and his family, 500 years ago? What would we see?

On the day that Brown Beaver returned from finding his guardian spirit, his family greeted him with great joy. His little sister, Mink Foot, was especially happy.

The family talked about other boys who had gone into the woods to pray for spirit helpers. All Caribou Hunter boys did this.

Mink Foot would not be likely to seek a guardian spirit. The people did not think women needed these spirits as much as men did. The Native people felt that women were already in tune with the spirits of nature. Mother earth gave

birth to new life, and so did the women when they had babies.

Brown Beaver's guardian spirit came in the form of a moose. Many other spirit helpers also came in the form of animals. Some came in the form of birds. Others took on human form.

Brown Beaver, Mink Foot, and their family lived in the northwestern part of what we now call Canada. They lived just south of the cold **Arctic**. Winters were long and cold. Summers were short and the ground was covered in bright wildflowers.

The area was so far north that not many trees grew. There were huge muskeg bogs. It was almost impossible to travel through the muskeg in the summer.

To live in their climate, Brown Beaver and Mink Foot had to learn many skills when they were very young. Mink Foot learned how to snare rabbits and other small animals. She learned to fish, and she learned to build fires.

In the winters, Mink Foot helped pull a toboggan. Her family used toboggans to carry their loads. They wore snowshoes to walk over the deep snow. In summer the people travelled either on foot or by canoe.

While Mink Foot and her mother pulled the toboggans, her father and Brown Beaver watched for game. The men were the main hunters. Brown Beaver liked to walk ahead and break the trail. He looked for animal tracks. How proud he was when he and some other hunters killed a bear with their bows and arrows!

It was not always easy for the Caribou Hunters to find food. Besides bear, they also hunted moose and smaller animals such as beaver. Their main food, though, was caribou meat. The caribou herds moved through the **barren** grounds in large numbers. However, no one could tell just when and where the herds would move.

1. How did the moose spirit say he would help Brown Beaver?

2. Some people call the area where Mink Foot and Brown Beaver lived the "land of little sticks." Do you think this name fits the area? Why?

3. How did Mink Foot and Brown Beaver spend most of their time as they were growing up?

Brown Beaver and Mink Foot's family never stayed long in one place. This is one reason why their homes were so simple. They set up a shelter by placing animal skins over pole frames. Sometimes they used strips of bark instead of animal skins to cover the frames. Sweet-smelling spruce boughs covered the floor. These helped to keep out the dampness and cold.

"It's time to make tea!" Mink Foot's mother often said after the family had set up their cone-shaped home. Mink Foot carefully heated stones in the fire. Then she dropped the hot stones into a pot of water. The stones heated the water. When the water was hot, she dropped in a piece of fungus from a birch tree. This was a special fungus that the Caribou Hunters used in making their kind of tea.

While they drank their tea, Mink Foot and her mother often worked on their sewing. They made shirts and leggings out of caribou skins. They **embroidered** the clothes with porcupine quills. They also made fringes and other decorations out of moose hair.

The Caribou Hunters lived in a way that made packing up and moving easy. They needed only a few tools: their stone or bone knives, scrapers, needles, and spoons for cooking.

Mink Foot and Brown Beaver grew up used to hard work. They spent many long winter evenings listening to stories. Sometimes their grandmother told stories that were so long it took several evenings to finish just one. This was the kind of story both children liked best.

Respect for Nature

All the groups of Native people had respect for nature. They believed that the different parts of the world are linked together. Do you think the Cree artist Jackson Beardy was thinking about this idea when he made this painting? How is the sun important to animals? How is water important?

The Caribou

Caribou meat was the most important food for Brown Beaver and his people. They used pounds to hunt the caribou. The pounds were much like those the Bison Hunters used to hunt bison. However, the Caribou Hunters' pounds were much bigger.

The people built a long hunting fence. It might stretch for many kilometres through the land. The fence was built in the shape of a funnel. At the narrow end was a round pound.

When the hunters found a herd of caribou, they drove them into the funnel. The herd ran along in front of the hunters. The animals' feet made strange clicking sounds.

At last the caribou entered the round pen. There the Caribou Hunters shot them with bows and arrows. Sometimes women and even children helped to shoot the caribou.

Then the people had fresh meat to eat. They had caribou hides to make their homes and clothing. The women dried some of the meat

to use for making pemmican. Pemmican kept a long time. It was good food for winter when fresh meat was scarce.

Pretend you are Mink Foot or Brown Beaver. Make up a short story about helping with a caribou hunt. Include in your story any interesting adventure you might have while going on the hunt.

1. Use the map on page 28 to find the homeland of the Inuit. Find this same area on a globe. The Far North is sometimes called "the roof of the world." Why do you think it has this name?

The Inuit

Okik was an Inuit boy who lived more than 500 years ago. He lived in one of the coldest climates in the world. In his homeland, north of the tree line, winters were nine months long.

Summer lasted only three months. Okik loved the long days when the sun never set. He and his people spent the summers inland, away from the coasts, to hunt caribou and **muskox**.

When the short summer ended and winter came, Okik's people moved back to the sea coasts. There they hunted sea mammals. They hunted polar bear, **walrus**, whale, and seal.

Okik was excited when he went on his first seal hunt. He went with his father. They drove their dog sledge up the coast some distance from camp. When they reached a good seal hunting area, Okik's father stopped the sledge. He and Okik walked out on the snow-covered ice along the sea coast. They took a dog with them—one that was very good at smelling.

Okik's father was looking for something. He was looking for an **agloo**. This is a tiny hole in the ice. It is a place where a seal might come up to breathe. Okik and his father hoped that the dog would be able to smell where a seal had been, and find an agloo.

All at once the dog trotted out on a flat stretch of ice beyond the bay. Nose down, it sniffed at the ice. Then it stopped. Okik was following close behind. His sharp eyes spotted something. It was an agloo.

Father sat down beside the little breathing hole. He began to get his harpoon ready. It was like a big spear. He had made it himself from the horn of a **narwhal**.

While Father got ready, Okik took the dog back to the sledge. When he returned to the agloo, he brought a long piece of sinew thread. He also brought some fluffy feathers —feathers from a snowy owl. Okik sat down near his father. He tied a feather to the end of the sinew thread.

Silently Father took the thread from Okik. He dropped

Raw Meat

Okik and his family got a lot of **vitamins** by eating their meat raw. Farther south, people get vitamins from plant foods such as fruit and vegetables. However, Okik and his people had almost no plant food, especially in the winter. They were wise to eat their meat raw. It helped keep them healthy and strong in a land of few food supplies.

1. Usually the only kind of wood the Inuit had was driftwood. This was wood that drifted to their shores from somewhere else. Why would driftwood be the only kind of wood they had?

74

the end of it into the hole. Then the two of them waited, and waited, and waited.

If the owl feather moved—even a little—it meant a seal had come. The animal's breath would make the feather flutter.

Nothing happened. Okik got tired of waiting. They waited even longer.

Suddenly the owl feather fluttered. Okik's father did not wait a moment. With all his might, he plunged his harpoon straight down into the agloo.

He got one! He got a seal! Okik felt happy. Tonight there would be a feast. He and Father would take the seal home on the sledge. Mother would skin it. She would cut the meat into tasty chunks.

Okik and his sister Mikak would run to tell the others in camp about the seal. Everybody would gather in their little turf house. Then the feast of raw seal meat would begin.

Daily Life

Okik and his people were very good at creating what they needed from whatever they could find around them. They usually made their sledges from whalebone or **driftwood**. What if they did not have these materials? Then they used whatever they did have.

One time Okik and his father had to use rolled caribou hides for sledge runners. For crosspieces, Okik suggested using long frozen fish. His idea worked! Laid side by side, the fish made a good top for the sledge.

The Inuit made their own boats as well. For hunting on water, Okik's father used a light one-person boat called a **kayak**. When the whole family was going somewhere, they used a larger skin boat called a **umiak**. Okik and Mikak loved to ride over the waves in the umiak.

In winter, snow was one material that Okik's people had lots of. From snow they could make a useful type of winter home. It was the **igloo**.

The Inuit did not live in igloos all the time. In fact, Okik's family seldom lived in one except when they were travelling in winter. For winter, the family built themselves a house of

The Seal-Oil Lamp

The drawing shows a lamp like the one that Okik's family used. The wick, some dried moss, had to be kept the right length so it wouldn't smoke. It was Okik's mother's job to tend the lamp. She used a flat stone to trim the wick. Mikak watched her mother carefully so she would learn how to do it.

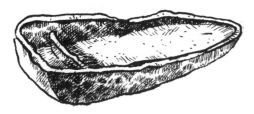

1. Look at the clothes you are wearing. Where did the materials come from to make them? Who made your clothes? Where did the material come from for Okik's clothes? Who made them?

turf. If they could not find enough turf around their winter camp, they used stones or driftwood. During the summer they lived in a caribou-skin tent that Okik's mother sewed.

Okik's mother also sewed all the family's clothes. The clothes for winter had to be very warm. Everyone in the family except the baby had to have stockings, boots, trousers, a shirt, and a **parka** of heavy fur. The baby had a one-piece suit of soft fur.

Stockings were made of deerskin and came over the knees. Boots were made of sealskin because it is oily and sheds water. Trousers were made of hide with the furry side turned in. Shirts and parkas were also made of fur. Okik's mother made the hood on her own parka very large. That is where she carried the baby. She trimmed the parkas with wolverine fur. When the wind blew, the long hairs protected the face.

Okik's mother had to keep the clothing well mended, too. She spent long winter evenings working on the family's clothing. While she was mending, Okik's father might carve a new lamp of whalebone. The small seal-oil lamps gave the family all the light and heat they needed for their winter home.

Okik's father and mother often told stories while they worked. Okik and Mikak liked to listen to stories late into the night until they fell asleep.

Inuit Boats

The boats the Inuit built were different from the canoes the other groups of Native Peoples used. The kayak was a boat made for one person. It was made of sealskin stretched over a frame of driftwood or bone. It was usually three to six metres long. The boat was all closed in except for a hole in the top. The hole was big enough for just one person. The Inuit used the kayak mainly to hunt seal or walrus.

The umiak was also made of bone or driftwood and sealskin. It was bigger than a kayak, usually nine to twelve metres long. It was an open boat that the Inuit used for their families. They also used the umiak for moving their belongings. Both of these boats were very light and could easily be carried when necessary.

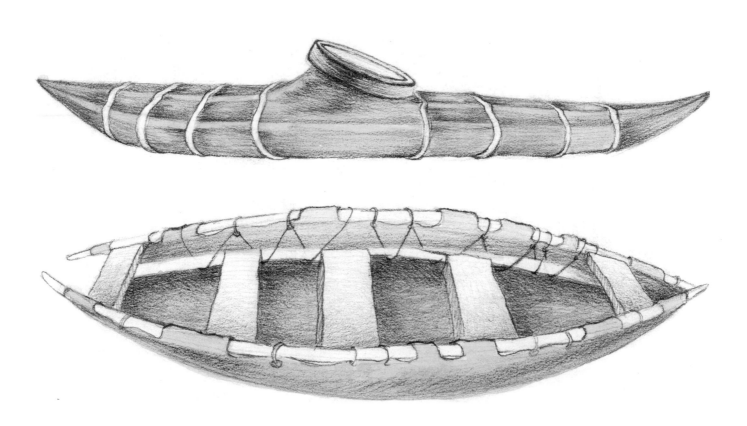

Animals of the North

Muskox

The muskox is well suited to life in the far North because it wears two coats. The outer coat is of long brown or black hair. The inner one is a cozy coat of wool. The Inuit hunted muskoxen for their warm coats and their tasty meat.

Seal

Many seal babies are born white. However, they soon shed their white coats and grow spotted ones. Seals are found in oceans all over the world, usually along the coasts. Seals are quick, smart animals, and are not easy to catch. The Inuit hunted seals for meat and for their skins.

Walrus

The walrus belongs to the same family as the seal. Unlike the seal, however, the walrus has tusks. It is also bigger than most seals.

The walrus is a strong swimmer. It feeds on fish. The Inuit hunted walruses for their meat, their skin, their oil, and the ivory in their tusks.

Narwhal

The narwhal is about the length of an average living room! It is a type of whale. The male narwhal has a single sword-like tusk. The Inuit found this tusk useful for making harpoons and other objects. They also hunted the narwhal for its meat and its hide, which they sometimes used to cover their umiaks.

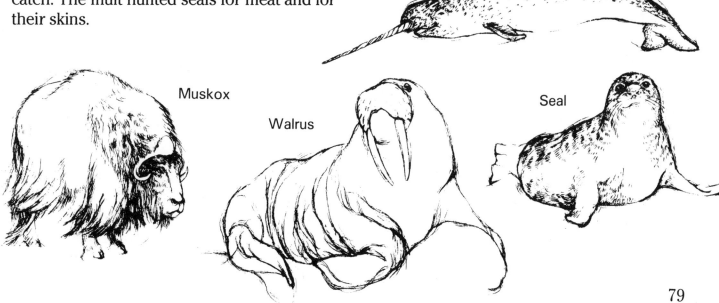

Narwhal

Muskox

Walrus

Seal

Glossary

ancestors Relatives such as parents, grandparents, and great-grandparents.

agloo The Inuit word for a small hole in the ice.

antelope An animal with hoofs and long horns. Looks like a small deer, but belongs to the same family as the goat.

Arctic The area around the North Pole and Arctic Ocean.

bannock A chewy kind of bread. Often it is flat and round.

barren Bare. Empty. Having few trees.

birchbark Bark from a slender tree called the birch. Birchbark is smooth. It is usually white.

bison A wild ox with a big shaggy head and short horns. Also called a buffalo.

bog A swamp or marsh. Soft, wet, spongy ground.

buckskin Deer skin.

camas A flowering plant that grows on the West Coast. The Plateau Peoples ate the camas roots.

caribou A large North American reindeer.

cedar An evergreen tree of the pine family.

clan A group of related families.

climate The kind of weather over a period of time. Includes wind, dryness and moisture, heat and cold.

community A group of people living close together.

co-operate To work together. To get along well together.

corral A closed-in space in which animals are caught or kept.

cougar A large wildcat. Golden brown in colour.

driftwood Wood floating in water or washed up on shore by water.

elk A large kind of deer with moose-like antlers.

embroider To decorate with a pattern of stitches.

explorer A person who travels to places to find out about them.

festival A special, joyful time. A feast.

flint A very hard kind of stone, brown or grey in colour.

fly swatter A tool for hitting and killing flies. Often has a long handle.

Friendship Centre A place where Native people can go to talk, relax, or get help with finding jobs or a place to live. Friendship Centres are run by Native people in most of the larger Canadian cities.

fringe A border of loose or bunched threads. May be found along the end of a piece of clothing.

fungus A plant that has no flowers or leaves or green colouring, like a mushroom.

game Wild animals, birds, or fish that people hunt or catch.

government The system of ruling. The form of control over a country or other area.

guardian spirit A spirit sent to help or protect a person.

hare An animal like a rabbit, but bigger. It has long ears, long hind legs, and a short tail.

herb A plant used in cooking or medicine. For instance, sage, mint, and parsley are herbs.

herd A large number of animals together.

igloo A dome-shaped house built out of blocks of snow. Used by the Inuit.

inlet A narrow strip of water running into a coastline from a larger body of water.

Inuit The group of Native people living the farthest North.

kayak A boat made by the Inuit for one person.

landscape A wide view of land. Scenery.

legend A story from the past. A legend may or may not be true. Often it involves a real person or place.

leggings Coverings for the legs, often made of leather.

longhouse The kind of dwelling built by the Corn Planters of the southeastern part of what is now Canada. Longhouses were made of pole frames covered with shingles. Each was big enough for several families.

lynx A wildcat with long legs, a short tail, and tufted ears.

marsh An area of soft wet land.

muskeg A swamp or marsh. An area of bog made up of rotting plants, especially mosses.

musk-ox A large shaggy animal of the Arctic; looks like a sheep and an ox.

narwhal A large Arctic whale. The male narwhal has a tusk.

nation A country. A land.

Native A person born in a certain area or country.

newcomer A person who has just arrived, or a person who arrived not long ago.

oolichan A small fish of the smelt family found on the Pacific coast. Also called a *candlefish*.

parka A very warm winter coat with a hood. The Inuit made their parkas of fur.

pemmican A mixture of dried meat and fat. Sometimes it included berries.

pipeline A long line of pipe used for moving oil, gas, water, or other liquid.

plateau A high plain, often found between ranges of mountains.

plywood A type of board made by gluing several thin layers of wood together.

potlatch A Pacific Coast gift-giving festival.

pound A closed-in area for trapping or keeping animals.

pow-wow A ceremony or meeting held by North American Native people.

rapids Parts of a river or stream where the water rushes quickly, often over rocks.

red ochre A reddish earth.

reserve A piece of land set aside for a group of Native people to use.

resourceful Good at thinking of ways to do things.

roach A headpiece made of deer hair.

sagebrush A grey-green shrub. Often grows in dry plains.

scarce Hard to get.

scout A person sent out to get information. Prairie Bison Hunters used scouts to find out where bison herds were.

settler A person who settles, or makes a home in a new land.

shingle A thin slab of wood or other material for covering a roof. Shingles are usually put on in rows that overlap.

sinew A strong tough cord, or band, that joins muscle to bone.

smallpox A disease that causes fever and sores on the skin.

smokestack A tall chimney, often seen on a factory.

snare To trap with a loop of rope.

spawn To produce eggs. To lay eggs.

spirit A being that cannot be seen. The Native people believed that spirits have certain powers.

spirit helper A guardian spirit who helps and protects a person.

Subarctic The area just south of the Arctic. In the Subarctic, winters are long and cold. Summers are short.

swamp A marsh. Soft wet land.

tipi A type of tent used by some Native peoples, especially on the western plains. Made of skins over a frame shaped like a cone.

totem An animal, plant, or other thing used as the sign of a Native family group or clan.

totem pole A pole carved and painted with totems.

trading post A store run by a trader. The Europeans set up trading posts to trade with the Native peoples.

travois A wooden platform used by the Bison Hunters of the prairies. It was made of two poles with a platform close to the ground for carrying a load.

treaty A formal agreement between groups of people.

tunic A loose garment like a shirt.

turf Sod. Grass with its matted roots.

umiak Boat made of sealskin and driftwood. Used by the Inuit.

vitamin Any of a number of substances needed for good health. Vitamins are found in foods. For instance, vitamin C is found in oranges.

vow To promise.

walrus A large sea mammal of the Arctic. A walrus is something like a seal, but has long tusks.

wampum Beads made from shells. In the past it was used as money by some Native groups.

weir A fence of stakes put in a river or stream to catch fish.

wigwam A type of tent used by the Eastern Woodland Hunters. Made of bark or skins over a frame shaped like a cone.

wrestling A sport in which two people try to throw or force each other to the ground.

Canadian Native Peoples Series

Titles in the Series:

1234567890/FP/0987654321